# A CENTURY OF LIFE GOALS

**"Empower Your Future: A Roadmap to Achievement Through One Hundred Life Goals"**

**By**

**"Ruben M. Gregory"**

# TABLE OF CONTENT

# INTRODUCTION

Introduction In the intricate tapestry of existence, "A Century of Life Goals" beckons you on a transformative journey. This title encapsulates the essence of intentional living, inviting you to navigate the labyrinth of aspirations and ambitions with a clear vision. Join the quest to shape a life of purpose, one goal at a time, as each carefully chosen milestone becomes a building block in the grand architecture of your unique and fulfilling journey.

# 1 SELF-GROWTH

**Reading self-help is a personal journey, and individuals choose these books based on their specific needs, interests, and goals. It's important to approach self-help literature with an open mind, recognizing that not every concept or piece of advice will resonate with everyone. The ultimate goal is to use the knowledge gained from these books to make positive changes and lead a more fulfilling life.**

**Clarify Your Healing Principles:** **Clarifying your principles in setting life goals involves taking the time to identify and articulate the fundamental values and beliefs that will guide your decision-making and actions. It's about understanding what truly matters to you, what you stand for, and what principles will**

serve as the foundation for the goals you set. By doing so, you create a clear framework that aligns your aspirations with your core values, providing a solid and meaningful direction for your life journey. This process helps ensure that your goals are not only achievable but also deeply connected to your principles, fostering a sense of purpose and fulfillment.

**Discover a Mentor:**
Seeking a mentor is a proactive step toward personal and professional growth.
Creating a power hour involves dedicating a specific block of time to focus on tasks that contribute significantly to your goals, productivity, and personal growth.

Here's a suggested framework for developing your power hour:

## Power Hour Framework

### Set a Specific Goal

Define a clear objective for your power hour. It could be related to work, personal development, fitness, or any other area you want to focus on.

### Prioritize Tasks:

Identify the most important and impactful tasks that align with your goal. These should be tasks that, when completed, move you closer to your objectives.

### Time Blocking:

Allocate a dedicated hour in your daily or weekly schedule for your power hour. Choose a time when you are typically most focused and energized.

### Eliminate Distractions:

Turn off notifications, close unnecessary tabs, and create a quiet, focused environment to minimize interruptions.

**Segment Your Time:**
Divide the hour into focused segments. For example, you might spend 20 minutes on a strategic work task, 20 minutes on learning or personal development, and 20 minutes on a physical activity.

**Rotation Method:**
Consider rotating the focus areas each day to ensure a well-rounded approach to your personal and professional development.

**Reflection:**
Reserve the last few minutes of your power hour for reflection. Review what you accomplished, assess your progress, and make notes for adjustments in future power hours.

**Consistency:**
Stick to your schedule and make your power hour a consistent part of your routine. Consistency is key to building momentum and seeing long-term benefits.

**Sample Power Hour Plan:**
**First 20 Minutes: Strategic Work Task (e.g., Priority Project)**
**Next 20 Minutes: Personal Development (e.g., Reading, Learning)**
**Last 20 Minutes: Physical Activity (e.g., Exercise, Stretching)**
**Feel free to customize the framework based on your goals, preferences, and daily schedule. The key is to make the most of this dedicated time to achieve meaningful results in various aspects of your life.**

**Enroll in a Learning Session.**
**you have to formally register or sign up for a scheduled educational or instructional event. This can include workshops, seminars, courses, or training sessions designed to provide participants with specific knowledge, skills, or insights in a particular subject area. By enrolling in such a session, individuals commit to attending and actively participating in the learning experience, often led by an expert or instructor. The goal is to**

acquire new information, enhance existing skills, or gain a deeper understanding of a specific topic. Enrolling in a learning session is a proactive step toward personal or professional development.

## Continuous Learning.

Continuous learning refers to the ongoing, intentional, and lifelong process of acquiring new knowledge, skills, and competencies. It involves a proactive approach to personal and professional development, emphasizing the idea that learning is not confined to specific periods or formal education. Instead, it becomes a part of one's daily life, allowing individuals to adapt to change, stay relevant in their fields, and foster a growth mindset.

Key elements of continuous learning include:
Adaptability: Embracing change and staying open to new ideas and perspectives.

**Self-Direction:** Taking responsibility for one's learning journey and setting personal goals.

**Curiosity:** Cultivating a natural curiosity and eagerness to explore new subjects.

**Informal and Formal Learning:** Engaging in both structured educational activities and informal learning experiences.

**Skill Development:** Focusing on acquiring practical skills that align with personal and professional aspirations.

**Continuous learning is increasingly recognized as essential in a rapidly evolving world, where staying competitive and adaptable requires a commitment to ongoing education and skill enhancement.**

**Developing a positive.**
**is a valuable aspect of personal growth and well-being.**
**Here are some strategies to cultivate and maintain a positive mindset:**

**Practice Gratitude:**
Regularly express gratitude for the positive aspects of your life. Consider keeping a gratitude journal.

**Positive Affirmations:**
Use positive affirmations to challenge and overcome self-sabotaging and negative thoughts.

**Surround Yourself with Positivity:**
Spend time with positive, supportive individuals who uplift and inspire you.
Focus on Solutions. Instead of dwelling on problems, focus on finding solutions and taking proactive steps.

**Learn from Challenges.**
View challenges as opportunities for growth and learning. Embrace a mindset of resilience.

**Limit Negative Inputs.**
Reduce exposure to negative news, toxic people, or situations that contribute to negativity.

**Mindful Awareness.**
Practice mindfulness to stay present and avoid unnecessary worries about the past or future.

**Celebrate Small Wins.**
Acknowledge and celebrate your achievements, no matter how small. It boosts confidence.

**Adopt a Growth Mindset.**
Embrace challenges as opportunities to learn and grow. See failures as stepping stones to success.

**Take Care of Yourself.**
Prioritize self-care, including adequate sleep, regular exercise, and a balanced diet.

**Visualize Success.**
Use visualization techniques to picture yourself succeeding in your goals and endeavors.

**Help Others.**
Acts of kindness and helping others can contribute to a sense of purpose and positivity.

**Learn Optimism.**
Challenge negative thoughts and reframe them in a more positive and constructive light.

**Engage in Positive Activities.**
Participate in activities that bring joy and fulfillment. Surround yourself with positivity.

**Keep Learning.**

Stay curious and continuously seek opportunities for learning and personal development.
Remember, developing a positive attitude is an ongoing process that

requires conscious effort and commitment. It involves changing habitual thought patterns and embracing a more optimistic outlook on life. Consistency in practicing these strategies can lead to a positive transformation in your mindset over time.

# 2 Developing effective communication skills.

is crucial for personal and professional success.

Here are strategies to enhance your communication abilities:

### Active Listening.

Pay full attention to the speaker, avoid interrupting, and provide feedback to demonstrate understanding.

### Empathy.

Understand and share the feelings of others. Put yourself in their shoes to better connect with their perspectives.

**Clear Articulation.**
Practice expressing your thoughts clearly and concisely. Avoid jargon and use language appropriate for your audience.

**Body Language.**
Be mindful of your non-verbal cues, including eye contact, facial expressions, gestures, and posture.

**Confidence.**
Believe in your ability to communicate effectively. Confidence enhances your message and encourages engagement.

**Adaptability.**
Tailor your communication style to fit different situations and audiences. Be flexible in your approach.

**Constructive Feedback.**
Provide feedback positively and constructively. Focus on specific behaviors and suggest improvements.

**Clarity in Writing.**
Practice writing clear and concise messages, whether in emails, reports, or other written forms.

**Cultural Awareness.**
Be mindful of cultural differences in communication styles. Adapt your approach to be culturally sensitive.

**Conflict Resolution.**
Develop skills in resolving conflicts peacefully. Focus on finding common ground and mutually beneficial solutions.

**Ask Questions.**
Seek clarification and encourage open dialogue by asking questions. This shows genuine interest in the conversation.

**Mindful Speech.**
Be conscious of your tone and pace of speech. Ensure that your verbal delivery aligns with your intended message.

**Public Speaking Practice.**
Practice public speaking regularly to build confidence and refine your presentation skills

**Networking.**
Engage in networking opportunities to practice conversational skills and build professional relationships.

**Learn from Others.**
Observe effective communicators, both in person and through media. Identify techniques you can incorporate into your style.

**Conflict Resolution Training.**
Attend workshops or training programs focused on conflict resolution and effective communication.

**Mindfulness and Presence.**
Practice being present in conversations. Minimize distractions and focus on the person or topic at hand.

Join Toastmasters or Similar Groups. Participate in groups that provide a supportive environment for improving communication and public speaking skills.

Remember, improving communication is an ongoing process. Consistent practice and a willingness to learn from each interaction contribute to continuous growth in this essential skill set.

# 3 Discovering spirituality :

is a personal and introspective journey that involves exploring your beliefs, values, and connection to something beyond the material world. Here are steps you can take to begin your exploration of spirituality.

### Reflect on Your Beliefs.

Take time to reflect on your beliefs about life, existence, purpose, and the nature of reality. Consider whether you identify with a particular religious tradition or if you have your unique spiritual perspective.

### Explore Different Traditions.

Read about various spiritual and religious traditions to gain a broader understanding of different perspectives. Attend services, visit places of worship, and engage in conversations with people from diverse spiritual backgrounds.

### Meditation and Mindfulness.

Practice meditation or mindfulness to cultivate a deeper connection with your inner self. These practices can help you become more aware of your thoughts, emotions, and the present moment.

### Connect with Nature.

Spend time in nature to experience a sense of awe and connection with the world around you. Nature can be a powerful source of spiritual inspiration.

### Read Spiritual Literature.

Explore books and literature on spirituality. This can include religious texts, philosophical writings, and works by spiritual teachers. Look for texts that resonate with your beliefs and values.

**Seek Guidance.**

If you're drawn to a specific spiritual tradition, seek guidance from mentors, teachers, or community leaders. They can provide insights and support as you navigate your spiritual journey.

**Attend Spiritual Events.**
Attend spiritual gatherings, workshops, or retreats. These events can provide opportunities for learning, self-discovery, and connecting with like-minded individuals.

**Practice Compassion and Gratitude.**
Cultivate compassion and gratitude in your daily life. Acts of kindness and expressions of gratitude can deepen your sense of connection with others and the world.

**Journaling.**
Keep a spiritual journal to document your thoughts, experiences, and insights. Writing can be a powerful tool for self-discovery.

**Question and Reflect.**
Continuously question and reflect on your beliefs. Consider how your spiritual understanding evolves over time and through different life experiences.

**Art and Creativity.**
Engage in creative activities that allow you to express your spiritual insights. This could include art, music, or writing.

**Connect with Community.**
Join a spiritual community or group where you can share and discuss your journey with others. Community support can be invaluable in the exploration of spirituality.

Remember that spirituality is a personal and evolving aspect of life. It's about finding meaning, purpose, and connection in a way that aligns with your deepest values. Take the time to explore, be open to new experiences, and allow your spirituality to unfold naturally.

# 4 PHYSICAL WELLBEING

**Creating and maintaining health and fitness for yourself involves adopting a holistic approach that encompasses physical activity, proper nutrition, adequate rest, and mental well-being. Here are some key steps to help you build a sustainable and personalized**

**health and fitness routine**
**Incorporating a health and fitness routine into your life can have a significant impact on your ability to set and achieve life goals. Here are several ways in which a healthy lifestyle can positively influence your overall well-being and success:**

**Increased Energy Levels:**
**Regular physical activity boosts your energy levels by improving cardiovascular health and circulation.**

With more energy, you'll be better equipped to tackle daily tasks and pursue your long-term goals with vigor.

### Enhanced Mental Clarity:

Exercise has been shown to have cognitive benefits, including improved focus, memory, and overall mental clarity. A healthy mind is better equipped to set and pursue ambitious life goals.

### Stress Reduction:

Engaging in physical activity helps reduce stress by triggering the release of endorphins, the body's natural stress relievers. A calm and focused mind is essential for effective goal-setting and problem-solving.

### Improved Mood and Motivation:

Exercise has a positive impact on mood by promoting the release of neurotransmitters like serotonin and dopamine. A more positive outlook on life can enhance your motivation and determination to achieve your goals.

### Enhanced Productivity:
Regular physical activity has been linked to increased productivity. When you are physically fit, you are more likely to stay focused and maintain high levels of productivity, making it easier to work towards your goals.

### Better Physical Health:
A healthy body is better equipped to handle the demands of life. Improved physical health reduces the likelihood of illnesses and provides a solid foundation for pursuing and achieving your long-term aspirations.

### Increased Self-Esteem and Confidence:
Achieving fitness goals can contribute to higher self-esteem and confidence. This positive self-image can spill over into other areas of your life, giving you the belief that you can overcome challenges and achieve your ambitions.

### Balanced Lifestyle:
Integrating health and fitness into your routine encourages a more balanced lifestyle. This balance can extend to other aspects of your life,

including work, relationships, and personal development.

### Long-Term Vision:
Regular exercise fosters a long-term perspective on health and well-being. This mindset can translate into your life goals, encouraging you to set goals with a focus on sustained success and well-being.

### Increased Resilience:
Regular exercise builds physical and mental resilience. When facing challenges in your life goals, this resilience can be a valuable asset, helping you bounce back from setbacks and persist in the face of adversity.

In summary, adopting a health and fitness routine can positively impact various aspects of your life, providing a solid foundation for setting and achieving ambitious life goals. A healthy body and mind contribute to increased energy, mental clarity, motivation, and overall well-being, creating an environment conducive to success and fulfillment.

## Set Clear Goals.
Define specific, measurable, and realistic health and fitness goals. Whether it's weight loss, muscle gain, improved endurance, or overall well-being, having clear objectives will guide your efforts.

**Start with Small Changes.**
Gradually introduce small, manageable changes to your lifestyle. This could include incorporating more fruits and vegetables into your diet, taking short walks, or practicing mindfulness.

**Regular Exercise.**
Include both cardiovascular exercises (e.g., walking, running, cycling) and strength training (e.g., weightlifting, bodyweight exercises) in your routine. Aim for at least 150 minutes of moderate-intensity aerobic activity per week, along with muscle-strengthening activities on two or more days.

**Balanced Nutrition.**
Focus on a balanced diet that includes a variety of nutrient-dense foods. Prioritize whole foods such as fruits, vegetables, lean proteins, whole grains, and healthy fats. Stay hydrated by drinking an adequate amount of water.

### Portion Control.

Be mindful of portion sizes to avoid overeating. Use smaller plates, listen to your body's hunger and fullness cues, and avoid distractions while eating.

### Adequate Rest and Recovery.

Ensure you get enough quality sleep each night. Quality sleep is crucial for physical and mental recovery. Allow your muscles time to recover between workouts to prevent burnout and reduce the risk of injury.

### Manage Stress.

Incorporate stress management techniques such as meditation, deep breathing exercises, yoga, or other activities that promote relaxation. Chronic stress can negatively impact both physical and mental health.

### Consistency is Key.

Consistency is crucial for seeing long-term results. Create a schedule that you can realistically stick to and gradually increase the intensity and duration of your workouts as your fitness level improves.

### Mix Up Your Routine.

Keep your workouts interesting by trying new activities or varying your exercise routine. This helps prevent boredom and ensures that you engage different muscle groups.

### Stay Hydrated.

Drink an adequate amount of water throughout the day. Water is essential for various bodily functions, including digestion, nutrient absorption, and temperature regulation.

### Regular Health Check-ups.

Schedule regular check-ups with your healthcare provider to monitor your overall health and address any potential issues early on. Social Support.

# 5 LOVE ONES

**Surround yourself with a supportive community or workout buddy. Having social support can positively impact your motivation and adherence to a healthy lifestyle.**

**the key is to create a sustainable and enjoyable health and fitness routine that aligns with your goals and fits into your lifestyle. It's not about perfection but rather making consistent, positive choices for your well-being.**

**Family and friends can have a significant impact on the process of creating and pursuing life goals. Here are various ways in which their influence may play a role:**

**Support and Encouragement. Positive support and encouragement from family and friends can boost your confidence and motivation. Knowing that you have a support**

system can make it easier to pursue challenging goals.

### Role Modeling.

Observing the achievements and experiences of family members and friends can serve as inspiration. Positive role models can provide insights into goal-setting, perseverance, and success.

### Feedback and Advice.

Seeking feedback and advice from those close to you can offer valuable perspectives. Family and friends may provide insights, suggestions, and constructive criticism that can refine your goals.

### Collaboration.

In some cases, shared goals or collaborative efforts with family and friends can strengthen relationships and create a sense of shared purpose.

### Networking Opportunities.

Connections with family and friends can open up networking opportunities, providing access to resources, mentorship, or introductions that align with your goals.

### Emotional Well-being.

Positive relationships contribute to emotional well-being, which is crucial for maintaining focus, resilience, and mental clarity as you work toward your life goals.

### Cultural and Social Influences.

Family and friends often play a role in shaping your values, beliefs, and cultural background. These influences can impact the types of goals you set and the paths you choose to pursue.

### Balancing Priorities.

Family and friends can provide insights into balancing personal and professional life. Their experiences may offer guidance on managing time, relationships, and responsibilities while working toward your goals.

### Motivation During Challenges.

During difficult times or setbacks, emotional support from family and friends can be a crucial motivator. Knowing that others believe in you can help you persevere through challenges.

### Shared Experiences.

Shared experiences with family and friends can create meaningful memories that contribute to your overall life satisfaction and sense of fulfillment.

### Cultural Expectations.

Cultural expectations within your family or social circles may influence the types of goals you set and the values you prioritize.

### Influence on Values.

Family and friends contribute to shaping your values and belief systems, influencing the choices you make in setting life goals.

While the impact of family and friends can be positive, it's essential to maintain autonomy in setting goals that align with your values and aspirations. Striking a balance between external influences and personal autonomy is key to creating meaningful and authentic life goals.

# 6 FUNDS

Finance plays a crucial role in shaping and achieving life goals. The impact of finance on life goals is multifaceted and can influence various aspects of your personal and professional aspirations.
Here are key ways in which finance can affect life goals:

## Goal Affordability.

The financial resources available often determine the feasibility of certain life goals. Adequate funds are required for education, homeownership, travel, starting a business, or other significant endeavors.

## Quality of Life.

Financial stability contributes to an improved quality of life, impacting factors such as housing, healthcare, education, and overall well-being.

**Education and Skill Development.**
Financial resources are essential for pursuing educational goals and skill development. They enable access to educational opportunities, courses, and training programs that can enhance career prospects.

**Career Advancement.**
Investing in professional development often requires financial resources. Pursuing additional certifications, attending conferences, or enrolling in courses can contribute to career growth and achievement of professional goals.

**Entrepreneurship and Business Goals.**
Starting and sustaining a business often involves significant financial investment. Access to capital is crucial for entrepreneurs pursuing business-related life goals.

Homeownership.
Purchasing a home is a common life goal that requires a substantial financial commitment. Factors such as saving for a down payment and securing a mortgage impact the ability to achieve this goal.

Travel and Experiences.
Financial resources influence the ability to travel and engage in enriching experiences. Whether it's exploring new destinations, attending cultural events, or pursuing hobbies, having the means to do so contributes to personal fulfillment.

Retirement Planning.
Financial planning is essential for achieving retirement goals. Adequate savings, investments, and a well-structured retirement plan contribute to a comfortable and secure retirement.

Health and Wellness.
Access to healthcare, fitness programs, and wellness initiatives often requires financial resources.

Prioritizing health-related goals may involve expenses such as gym memberships, healthcare premiums, and nutritious food choices.

**Emergency Preparedness.**
Financial preparedness is crucial for unexpected events. Having an emergency fund and insurance coverage helps mitigate the impact of unforeseen circumstances on life goals.

**Debt Management.**
Managing and reducing debt is integral to achieving financial goals. High levels of debt can impede progress toward other life aspirations.

**Philanthropy and Giving Back.**
Financial stability enables individuals to contribute to causes they care about. Philanthropic goals, such as supporting charities or community initiatives are often linked to financial capacity.

**Family and Future Planning.**
Financial resources are central to family planning, whether it involves having children, providing for their education, or ensuring financial security for future generations.

**Lifestyle Choices.**
Financial considerations influence lifestyle choices, such as the decision to pursue a certain standard of living, live in a specific location, or engage in certain leisure activities.

Understanding the interplay between finance and life goals is essential for 6effective goal setting and planning. It involves managing resources wisely, making informed financial decisions, and aligning financial strategies with long-term aspirations.

# 7 LINES OF WORK

The choice of a career can have a profound impact on the creation and pursuit of life goals.
Here are several ways in which a career can influence one's life goals:

**Financial Stability.**
The income generated from a career can significantly impact one's ability to achieve financial goals, such as homeownership, travel, or investment in personal and professional dcvclopment.

**Professional Development.**
A chosen career path may offer opportunities for skill development, training, and advancement, aligning with professional goals and aspirations.

### Time Commitment.

The time demands of a career can affect the time available for pursuing personal goals. Balancing work and personal life is crucial for achieving a well-rounded set of objectives.

### Passion and Fulfillment.

A career that aligns with personal interests and passions can contribute to a sense of fulfillment and satisfaction, positively impacting overall life satisfaction.

### Networking Opportunities.

Certain careers provide extensive networking opportunities, facilitating connections that can contribute to achieving both professional and personal goals.

### Entrepreneurship and Innovation.

Individuals in entrepreneurial careers may have the opportunity to shape their businesses and work toward innovative goals.

**Impact on Health and Well-being.**
The nature of a career, including factors like work environment and stress levels, can impact overall health and well-being, influencing the pursuit of health-related life goals.

**Learning and Growth.**
Careers that offer continuous learning and growth opportunities contribute to personal development and the achievement of lifelong learning goals.

**Geographic Influence.**
Some careers may require relocation or involve travel, influencing lifestyle choices and impacting personal goals related to location or cultural experiences.

**Social Impact.**
Careers in fields such as social work, healthcare, or nonprofit organizations can contribute to achieving personal goals related to making a positive impact on society.

### Work-Life Balance.
The level of work-life balance afforded by a career can influence the ability to pursue personal goals, such as spending time with family, pursuing hobbies, or engaging in leisure activities.

### Retirement Planning.
The nature of a career, including retirement benefits and pension plans, can impact long-term retirement goals and financial security.

### Community Engagement.
Certain careers may provide opportunities for community engagement and social involvement, aligning with personal goals related to community service or social responsibility.

### Job Satisfaction.
Job satisfaction can contribute to overall life satisfaction and influence personal goals related to happiness and well-being.

**Career Transitions.**

**Changes in career paths or transitions between industries may impact the pursuit of new goals and the exploration of different interests.**

**It's important to align your career choices with your values, passions, and life goals. Regular self-assessment and reflection can help ensure that your career is a positive and supportive force in achieving a fulfilling and well-rounded life.**

# 8 VENTURES

Engaging in adventures can have a significant impact on the creation and pursuit of life goals. Here are various ways in which adventures can influence one's aspirations and overall life journey:

Personal Growth and Development. Adventures often push individuals out of their comfort zones, fostering personal growth, resilience, and the development of new skills. This growth can positively influence the pursuit of broader life goals.

Expanded Perspectives. Adventures expose individuals to new environments, cultures, and perspectives. This expanded worldview can inspire broader life goals.

### Increased Confidence.

Overcoming challenges and navigating unfamiliar situations during adventures can boost confidence. This newfound confidence can translate into a willingness to tackle ambitious life goals.

### Mindset Shifts.

Adventures can lead to shifts in mindset, encouraging individuals to embrace a more adventurous and open approach to life. This mindset can impact goal-setting by fostering a willingness to take calculated risks.

### Enhanced Problem-Solving Skills.

Facing uncertainties and solving problems during adventures hone problem-solving skills. These skills can be applied to overcome obstacles and challenges in the pursuit of life goals.

### Health and Well-being.

Participating in physical adventures, such as hiking or outdoor activities, contributes to overall health and well-being. A healthy lifestyle is often conducive to sustained energy and focus on life goals.


New Interests and Passions. Adventures can spark new interests and passions. These newfound passions may influence the creation of life goals, leading individuals to pursue activities aligned with their evolving interests.
Building Resilience. Adventures involve dealing with uncertainties and unexpected situations. Developing resilience during adventures can prepare individuals to navigate setbacks and challenges in the pursuit of life goals.

Cultivating Creativity. Exposure to novel experiences and environments can stimulate creativity. A creative mindset can influence innovative thinking and problem-solving in the pursuit of personal and professional goals.

**Strengthened Relationships.**
Shared adventures with friends, family, or partners can strengthen relationships. Supportive relationships often play a crucial role in achieving life goals.

**Sense of Accomplishment.**
Accomplishing challenging feats during adventures provides a sense of achievement. This sense of accomplishment can instill confidence and motivation to tackle ambitious life goals.

**Connection to Nature.**
Adventures in natural settings can foster a deeper connection to nature. This connection may influence life goals related to environmental sustainability, conservation, or outdoor pursuits.

**Inspiration for New Goals.**
Adventures can inspire individuals to set new goals, whether it's conquering specific challenges, learning new skills, or embarking on further adventures.

**Time Management Skills.**
Planning and executing adventurous activities require effective time management. These skills can transfer to the effective organization and pursuit of broader life goals.

**Increased Adaptability.**
Adventures often involve adapting to changing circumstances. This adaptability can be valuable in navigating uncertainties and changes when pursuing life goals.
Incorporating adventurous experiences into life can contribute to a rich tapestry of experiences, skills, and perspectives, ultimately shaping and enhancing the pursuit of meaningful life goals.

# 9 TRAVEL

Traveling can have a profound impact on the creation and pursuit of life goals. Here are various ways in which travel can influence one's aspirations and overall life journey:

## Cultural Awareness.

Exposure to different cultures during travel fosters cultural awareness and understanding. This expanded worldview can influence life goals by encouraging a more inclusive and globally-minded perspective.

## Personal Growth.

Travel often involves stepping out of one's comfort zone, leading to personal growth, increased self-confidence, and a greater sense of resilience. These qualities can positively impact the pursuit of ambitious life goals.

### Broadened Perspectives.

Experiencing diverse landscapes, lifestyles, and traditions broadens perspectives. This exposure can inspire individuals to set goals that reflect a more enriched and varied life.

### New Interests and Passions.

Travel exposes individuals to new activities, cuisines, and environments. It can spark new interests and passions that may influence the creation of life goals aligned with these newfound fascinations.

### Language Acquisition.

Visiting different regions often involves exposure to various languages. Learning new languages or enhancing language skills can open up opportunities and impact career-related life goals.

### Inspiration for Creativity.
Travel can be a source of inspiration for creative endeavors. Exposure to new art, architecture, and landscapes can stimulate creativity and influence the pursuit of creative life goals.

### Building Relationships.
Travel provides opportunities to meet new people and build relationships. These connections can have a lasting impact on personal and professional goals.

### Learning and Education.
Educational travel, whether formal or informal, exposes individuals to diverse educational experiences. This can influence life goals related to continuous learning, skill development, or academic achievements.

### Career Opportunities.
Travel may present career opportunities, especially in industries such as tourism, international business, or diplomacy. Expanding

one's professional horizons through travel can impact career-related life goals.

**Environmental Awareness.**
Experiencing different ecosystems and natural wonders can foster environmental awareness. This awareness may influence life goals related to environmental conservation and sustainability.

**Adventurous Spirit.**
Travel often involves a spirit of adventure and exploration. Developing an adventurous mindset can positively impact the pursuit of challenging and unconventional life goals.

**Networking.**
Traveling provides opportunities to network with people from various backgrounds and industries. These connections can influence career-related and personal life goals.

**Stress Reduction.**
Travel can be a means of relaxation and stress reduction. Managing stress positively impacts mental well-being and the ability to focus on and pursue life goals.

**Tolerance and Open-mindedness.**
Exposure to diverse cultures fosters tolerance and open-mindedness. These qualities can influence life goals by promoting inclusivity, understanding, and collaboration.

**Reflective Time.**
Travel often offers moments of reflection and self-discovery. This self-awareness can influence the setting of meaningful and authentic life goals.

Incorporating travel experiences into life can contribute to a more enriched, diverse, and fulfilling journey, shaping and influencing the pursuit of meaningful life goals.

# 10 LIFESTYLE.

The lifestyle one adopts can have a significant impact on the creation and pursuit of life goals. Here are various ways in which lifestyle choices can influence one's aspirations and overall life journey:

### Health and Well-being.
Adopting a healthy lifestyle, including regular exercise and a balanced diet, contributes to overall well-being. Good health positively influences the ability to pursue and achieve life goals.

### Time Management.
Efficient time management is a key component of many successful lifestyles. An organized and well-managed schedule can enhance productivity and contribute to achieving both personal and professional goals.

### Financial Habits.

Financial choices and habits shape one's lifestyle. Responsible financial management can provide the resources needed to pursue various life goals, from travel and education to homeownership and retirement.

### Work-Life Balance.

Striking a healthy balance between work and personal life is crucial. A balanced lifestyle supports the pursuit of personal goals, including spending time with family, pursuing hobbies, and engaging in leisure activities.

### Mindfulness and Stress Management.

Incorporating mindfulness practices and stress management techniques into one's lifestyle promotes mental well-being. A calm and focused mindset positively influences goal-setting and attainment.

**Sustainable Living.**
Adopting a sustainable lifestyle that minimizes environmental impact may influence life goals related to environmental conservation and sustainability.

**Social Connections.**
Building and maintaining strong social connections is a key aspect of lifestyle. Positive relationships contribute to emotional well-being and can provide support in the pursuit of life goals.

**Learning and Personal Development.**
A lifestyle that prioritizes continuous learning and personal development can influence the types of goals one sets. Lifelong learning and skill enhancement become integral parts of the journey.

**Travel and Exploration.**
A lifestyle that includes travel and exploration exposes individuals to diverse experiences and perspectives. This exposure can inspire a broader range of life goals, including those

related to cultural enrichment and personal growth.

### Creativity and Expression.
A lifestyle that encourages creativity and self-expression can influence the pursuit of creative and artistic life goals. Engaging in creative pursuits becomes an integral part of one's identity.

### Minimalism and Simplicity.
Embracing a minimalist or simplified lifestyle may influence life goals by prioritizing experiences and relationships over material possessions. This can lead to a focus on meaningful and purposeful pursuits.

### Entrepreneurial Mindset.
An entrepreneurial lifestyle, characterized by a proactive and risk-taking mindset, may influence career and business-related life goals. It fosters a willingness to innovate and take calculated risks.

**Cultural and Social Involvement.**
Active involvement in cultural and social activities becomes part of a lifestyle. This involvement can influence life goals related to community engagement, social impact, and philanthropy.

**Technology Integration.**
The integration of technology into one's lifestyle can impact the pursuit of life goals. It may involve leveraging digital tools for productivity, online learning, or networking.

**Self-Care Practices.**
Prioritizing self-care practices, such as regular exercise, sufficient sleep, and self-reflection, contributes to overall well-being. A healthy and balanced lifestyle supports the pursuit of meaningful life goals.
In essence, lifestyle choices serve as the backdrop against which life goals are set and pursued. Adopting a lifestyle aligned with one's values and

aspirations can create a supportive environment for the realization of meaningful and fulfilling life goals.

## Contributions to Posterity.

The impact of giving back or creating a legacy on life goals can be profound and multi-faceted. Here are several ways in which leaving a positive legacy or engaging in philanthropy can influence an individual's life goals:

## Sense of Purpose.

Contributing to a cause or leaving a positive legacy can provide a deep sense of purpose and fulfillment. It adds a meaningful dimension to life goals, aligning them with a greater sense of societal or community impact.

## Long-lasting Impact.

Building a legacy ensures that the impact of one's actions extends beyond their lifetime. This can be a powerful motivator, encouraging individuals to set goals that have enduring positive effects.

**Community Connection.**
Giving back fosters a sense of connection to the community or society. This connection can influence life goals by emphasizing the importance of collective well-being and shared responsibility.

**Positive Influence on Others.**
Leaving a legacy sets an example for others. The desire to positively influence and inspire others can become a driving force behind personal and professional life goals.

**Values Alignment.**
A commitment to giving back often reflects one's core values. Aligning life goals with these values ensures a more authentic and purpose-driven pursuit of aspirations.

**Enhanced Well-being.**
Engaging in philanthropy and leaving a legacy is associated with increased well-being and happiness. This positive mindset can spill over into other areas of life, influencing the

pursuit of personal and professional goals.

### Cultivation of Leadership Skills.
Taking on philanthropic initiatives often involves leadership roles. The skills developed in managing and leading such efforts can contribute to the achievement of leadership-related life goals.

### Expanded Perspective.
Giving back often involves addressing societal or global issues, and expanding one's perspective beyond individual concerns. This broader viewpoint can influence the types of goals set, incorporating elements of social responsibility and impact.

### Creating a Positive Reputation.
Leaving a positive legacy contributes to building a strong personal or professional reputation. This reputation can open doors and opportunities aligned with various life goals.

**Philanthropic Networks.**
Engaging in philanthropy often involves connecting with like-minded individuals and organizations. These networks can provide support, resources, and collaboration opportunities that align with specific life goals.

**Educational Pursuits.**
Legacy-building may involve supporting educational initiatives. This can influence life goals by emphasizing the value of education and learning, potentially influencing career choices and personal development goals.

**Generational Impact.**
Creating a legacy can extend to positively impacting future generations. This can shape life goals by emphasizing the importance of considering the long-term consequences of one's actions and decisions.

**Personal Growth and Reflection.**
The process of giving back often involves personal growth and self-reflection. This introspection can lead to the identification of more authentic and personally meaningful life goals.

**Legacy Planning.**
Actively planning and working toward leaving a legacy involves strategic thinking and goal-setting. This approach can influence how an individual approaches and prioritizes various life goals.

**Spiritual or Ethical Alignment.**
For some, giving back and leaving a legacy is tied to spiritual or ethical beliefs. Aligning life goals with these beliefs can provide a strong foundation for goal-setting and achievement.

In summary, giving back and creating a positive legacy can serve as a guiding principle that influences the nature and direction of an individual's life goals, contributing to a more purposeful and fulfilling life journey.

# CONCLUSION

"As you reach the final pages of 'a century of life goals,' remember that this isn't just a book—it's your guide to a profound transformation. Each target you've carefully outlined is a step towards self-realization, a beacon guiding you through the maze of life's possibilities. As the ink dries on your aspirations, embrace the power of intentionality and commitment. Your journey is not just about the goals; it's about the person you become along the way. So, stand tall amidst your dreams and let the echoes of your targets reverberate in every decision. This is your story, meticulously crafted with purpose and resilience—a testament to the extraordinary life you've designed."